Second-Hand Style

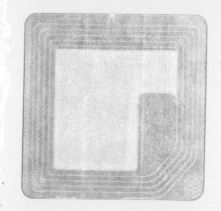

Editor, English-language edition: Matthew Giles
Designer Coordinator, English-language edition: Tina Thompson

Library of Congress Control Number: 2001133128
ISBN 0-8109-1226-0

Printed and bound in
10 9 8 7 6 5 4 3 2 1

Harry N. Abrams, Inc.
100 Fifth Avenue
New York, N.Y. 10011
www.abramsbooks.com

Abrams is a subsidiary of

LA MARTINIÈRE
GROUPE

Second-Hand Style

FINDING AND RENEWING ANTIQUE TREASURES

Design and Styling by
cRis Dupouy

Photographs by CHRISTOPHE MADAMOUR

Illustrations by BERTRAND CURE

Translated from the French by Molly Stevens

Harry N. Abrams, Inc., Publishers

Preface

This book invites you to consider the world differently. It invites you to wander through the world.... We fill objects with our desires and wishes. By transforming or reinterpreting them, we assert our individuality, our desire to create a magical oasis in our everyday lives.

When we rummage through a yard sale or a secondhand store, we're sharpening our eye, and learning how to make our homes our own. Culture and childhood memories come together, sprinkling these pages with magical sequins, carrying us away in a whirlwind of color: absinthe green and artist Yves Klein's famous hue, International Klein Blue, turquoise, and purple. There is no period furniture here, no big designers: only things you fall in love with for that special place in your home.

Use this book as inspiration and encouragement to come up with your own ideas, and when you're out perusing the flea markets and secondhand stores, you'll find yourself recognizing the potential in all you see around you. So, take up your brushes, and may the joy of antique-hunting, or making something into something else, be with you as you read these pages.

cRis Dupouy

Table of Contents

Tools and Tips

TOOLS

The implements we'll be using are essentially the simple tools in a basic toolbox:

- Drill
- Hammer
- Nails or tacks
- Brass wire
- Glue
- Paintbrushes
- Screwdriver
- Scraper to clean surfaces
- Wood-burning pen
- A pair of scissors
- Pliers

To this list add the stencils that you'll find in large hardware stores or specialized shops. But you can also make them yourself. Simply choose a motif, enlarge it if you need to on a copy machine, trace it, and transfer it on to Rhodoid.

MATERIALS

Paint

Preferably, choose paint that dries quickly and apply very thin coats to avoid dripping. Spray paint might help you save time. Also think about buying any appropriate paint thinners.

Gilding

On several occasions in this book, we'll be using copper leaf, which is similar to gold leaf, but a lot less expensive. It comes in a book and can be bought in art supply stores. You can also use small jars of model paint (for small surfaces) or gold spray paint.

Resin

For three of the objects, we will be using Cernit or Fimo polymer clay, which you bake. You'll find it in hobby shops. This plastic clay is easy to model and hardens when baked in the oven at between 250 and 300° F for about twenty minutes.

Supplies

You'll find beads, feathers, pendants, tips, and buttons either in hobby shops or by rummaging throughout the year in secondhand stores and yard sales.

Trims

Trims can easily be found at flea markets or specialized antiques dealers. However, there are also many notions stores that have a wider selection of new, very good quality products.

For your other materials, the idea is to salvage. Keep a lookout on your travels, and you're bound to find stuff that you'll want to use later. Collect your curiosities, treasures, and trimmings, store them away, and you'll have them when inspiration strikes.

HUNTING FOR ANTIQUES

Finding a flea market is as easy as looking in the newspaper. Flea-market shopping is a great weekend activity, and during the spring and summer seasons, yard sales pop up in many neighborhoods, offering all kinds of stuff at rock-bottom prices. Specialized publications sold at your local bookstore will give dates for upcoming fairs and yard sales, and FleaMarketGuide.com (http://www.FleaMarketGuide.com) is a great online resource for flea market locations across the U.S.

Brightening up…

Soft lighting, bright colored tulle, sparkly pendants, and fluffy feathers …

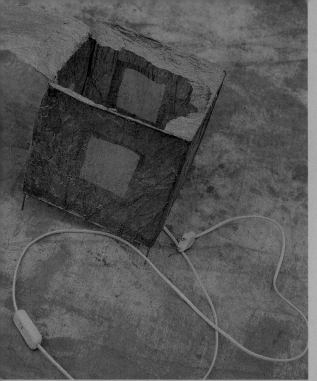

Materials
- 1 wire lamp
- 3 yards of tulle in the color of your choice
- Small butterfly clips
- 1 calico paper garland that matches the tulle

Butterfly Lamp

THESE LITTLE LAMPS, MADE BY PLACING

PAPER ON THE FLOOR, ARE OFTEN VERY

FRAGILE. IF THE ARMATURE ISN'T DAMAGED,

YOU CAN COVER IT IN A FEW YARDS OF

TULLE AND HOLD IT TOGETHER WITH

BUTTERFLY CLIPS.

Directions
- Make a ruffle of tulle around the wire armature. Attach with clips.
- Wrap the matching calico garland around the electrical wiring to hide it.

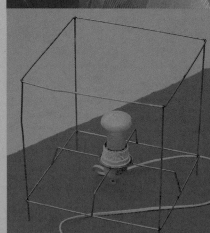

16

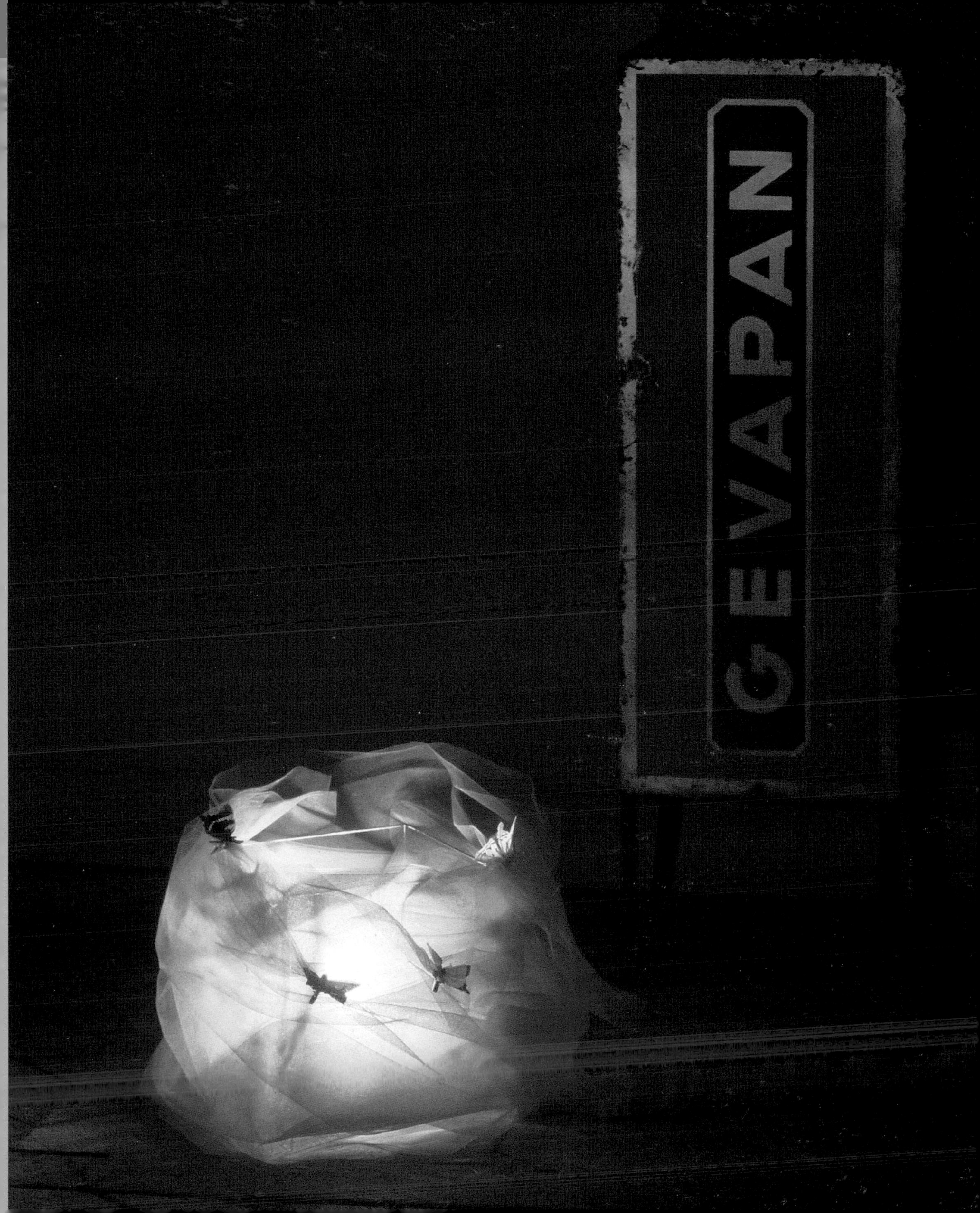
CEVAPAN

Moroccan Lamp

YOU CAN EASILY FIND THIS

KIND OF EASTERN LAMP

AT A FLEA MARKET.

PERSONALIZE IT WITH A

STRING OF CHRISTMAS

LIGHTS. PUT IT IN A RUSTIC

WOODEN BOWL WITH

COFFEE BEANS AND YOUR

HOUSE WILL SMELL GREAT.

A Short History of the Feather

From prehistoric times to the present day, feathers have continually been used for decoration. In many civilizations, from North America to the South Sea Islands, from pre-Columbian cities to Africa, feathers have been considered a symbol of virility, power, and sovereignty.

In Europe, feathers appeared in ornamentation starting in the Middle Ages. But it was especially during the Renaissance and the Belle Epoque that they had their greatest influence in interior decoration and fashion. As early as the sixteenth century, feather artisans formed guilds and, under the aegis of their patron, Saint George, they fabricated ornaments and accessories with feathers. Feathers were put forward in every era, with every fashion, but it was the ostrich feather that time and time again was the choice of stylish women. After the French Revolution, during the period of the *Incroyables* (1790), the fine ladies would style their hair with feathers day and night. At the end of the nineteenth century wonderful fans were used to add a final touch to a dress, and during the Belle Epoque, splendid boas were wrapped around bare necks and shoulders. Today, partly in the name of protecting animals, the use of feathers is dying out. The art is now applied mainly in fashion, interior decoration, and theatre.

TIME: 5 HOURS

Candlesticks with Pearls

I MADE THESE DELICATE CANDLESTICKS TO ADORN A MAGNIFICENT

EIGHTEENTH-CENTURY FIREPLACE. RAW AND BARE TO BEGIN WITH,

I TRANSFORMED THEM WITH FINE PEARLS AND FEATHERS.

Materials

- Candlesticks
- Brass wire
- Small silvery pearls
- Small bluish pearls
- Small chandelier cabochons
- Black rooster feathers
- Tips
- White paint
- Pliers

Directions

- Assemble the candlesticks and paint them white (see figure 1).
- Put two tips on brass wire, thread the feathers inside and, using your pliers, crush the tips so that they are secured (see figure 2). Thread a large Baroque cultured pearl and then thread about 2 feet of pearls and feathers however your inspiration leads you.
- Cut a second piece of wire measuring about 10 inches.
- Take a cabochon, loop the wire through it, place the tip, and crush with pliers. Continue however your inspiration leads you. End with a cabochon. (see figure 3).
- Wrap the shorter thread around the candlestick. Arrange the other on top.

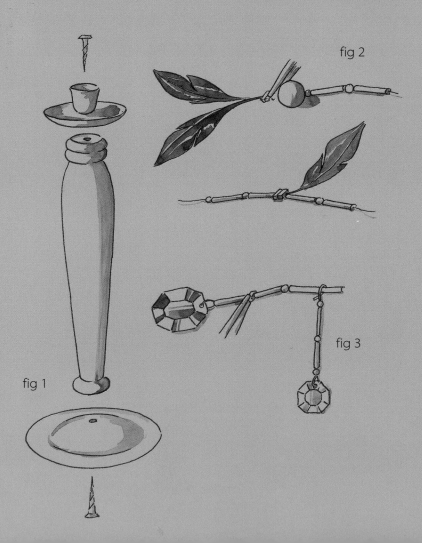

fig 2

fig 3

fig 1

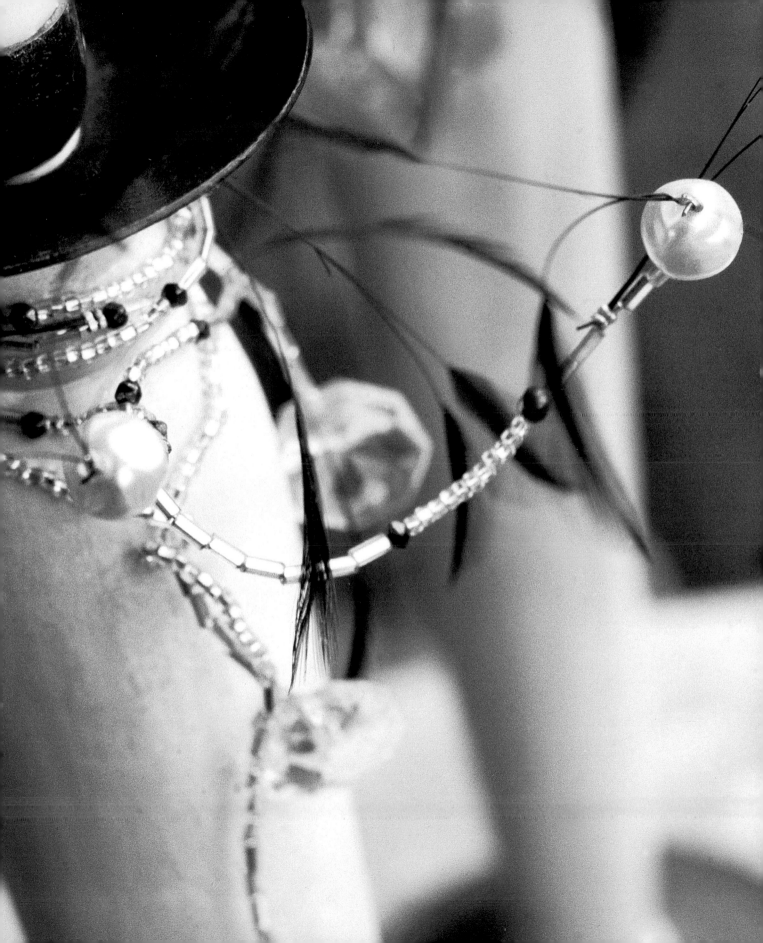

Chinese Lamp

THE PENDANTS ARE WHAT MAKES THIS PIECE CHIC. BECAUSE OF THEM, WE CAN TRANSFORM A CLASSIC LAMPSHADE INTO A PERSONAL CREATION. THE COLORS OF THE DIFFERENT ELEMENTS MATCH THE COLOR OF THE ORIGINAL LAMP BASE.

Materials

- 1 lamp base
- 1 lampshade
- Antique trimming ribbon
- Turquoise beads
- Small cultured pearls
- Small bronze-color beads
- Tips
- Blue and green feathers
- 1 artificial grasshopper
- Head pins
- Brass wire
- Red spray paint
- 1 drill
- Pliers
- Glue

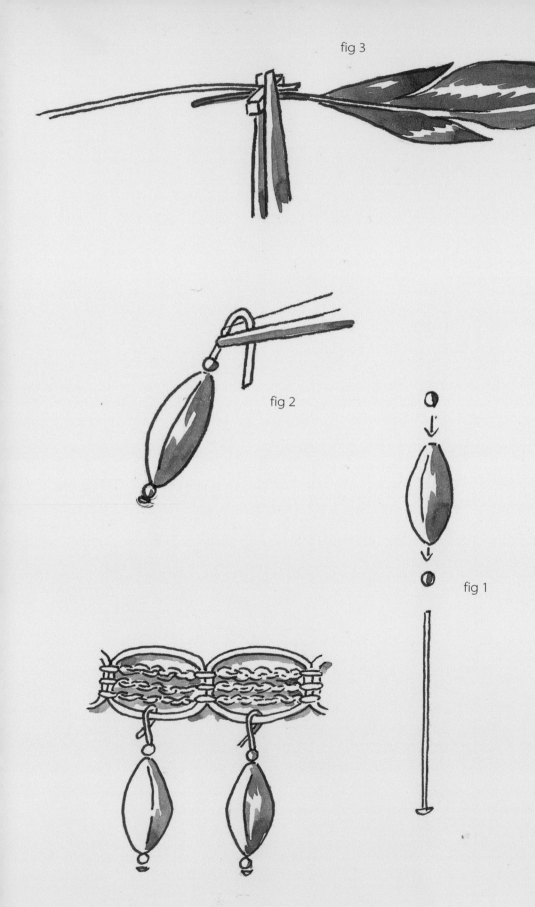

fig 3

fig 2

fig 1

Directions

- Take apart the lamp base. Spray-paint the parts that were initially wood color. Apply two or three coats.
- Do the same with the lampshade.
- Using the drill, make holes every quarter inch along the bottom rim of the lampshade.
- On the head pin, thread a cultured pearl, a turquoise bead, and then another cultured pearl. Then loop the pin with your pliers (see figures 1 and 2).
- Hook the piece into the lampshade hole and close the loop with your pliers. Repeat until you've gone around the lampshade.
- Cover the entire rim with antique braided trim.
- Drill a hole at the top of the lampshade.
- Cut three pieces of brass wire to different lengths. Put a tip on each. Thread a green or blue feather inside. Crush with your pliers (see figure 3), and then string the small bronze beads.
- When you have finished stringing the three wires, thread them through the drilled hole, bring together in a tip, and crush with your pliers.
- Glue braided trim around the top rim and add the artificial grasshopper.

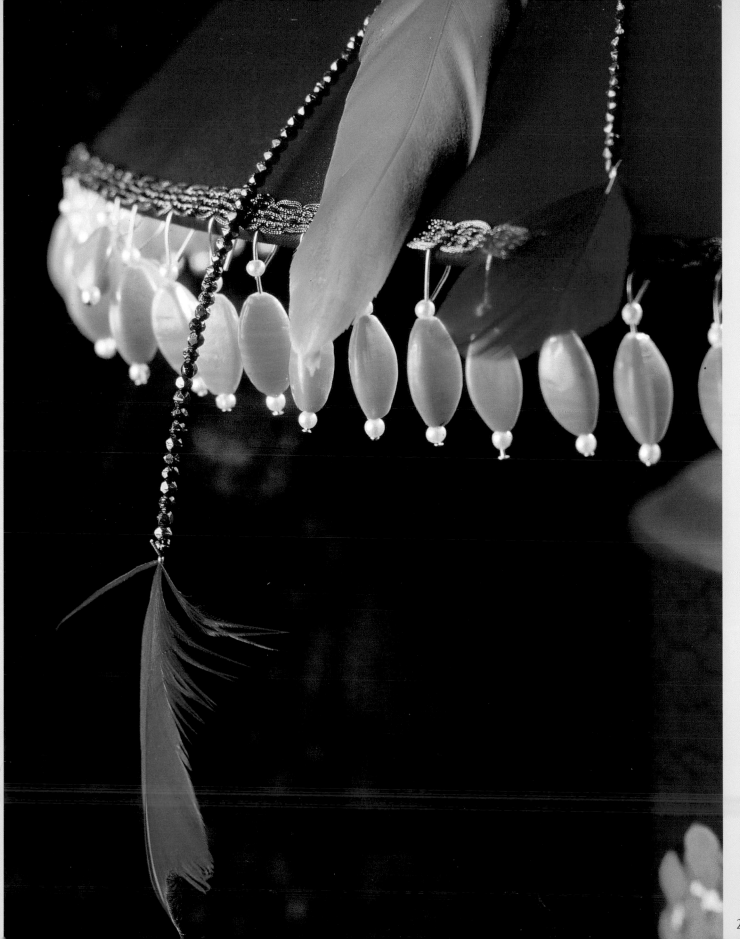

Feathered Candelabrum

WITH AN EVERYDAY WROUGHT IRON CANDELABRUM, A BIG EMMAUS CLASSIC, ALL YOU NEED IS SOME GOLD PAINT, SOME SPARKLES AND ROOSTER FEATHERS AND YOU'LL TRANSFORM THE ORDINARY INTO EASTER MAGIC.

Materials
- 1 wrought iron candlestick
- 2 feet of rooster feathers sold by the yard, strung and stitched
- Gold spray paint
- Glue

Directions

- Spray paint the wrought iron candlestick gold. Let dry.
- Glue the bottom of the small dishes and arrange the string of feathers. Cut off the excess.

33

A Short History of Glass

The first glass receptacles could be found in Egypt and Mesopotamia at the end of the sixteenth and beginning of the fifteenth century B.C. At this time, the pieces were probably carved from a block of hardened glass or perhaps were cast by artisans.

Blown glass emerged at the beginning of the Christian era between the first and fourth centuries A.D. The glass industry grew during the powerful Roman Empire all around the Mediterranean basin and therefore glass objects played an important role in everyday life. Certain decoration techniques developed at this time were so refined that they remain a mystery today. After the fall of Byzantium in the thirteenth century, Venice adopted eastern glass techniques. Since Murano, glass exports (beads, jewelry, stones, etc.) have won Venice fortune and fame. During the sixteenth century, Venetian glass and crystal were internationally known and coveted by other countries. Bohemia provided competition, fabricating a thicker material—in contrast to the delicacy of Italian glass— that allowed for deeper engraving and larger size. During the eighteenth century, France took over with the Baccarat, Saint-Louis and Sèvres glassworks factories. It was also at this time that the English invented faceted pendants for chandeliers and candelabras that would accentuate candlelight with their reflections.

The pendants or drops used in this book at one time hung from chandeliers, forming garlands and cascades.

Baroque Chandelier

WITH GOLD PAINT AND PENDANTS, YOU'LL MAKE A 1950s LANTERN

INTO A BAROQUE CHANDELIER.

Materials
- 1 1950s wall lamp
- 1 incomplete set of pendants
- Brass wire
- Tips
- 1 flat cabochon
- 1 faceted cabochon
- 1 votive candle
- Gold spray paint

Directions

- Remove the lamp's wiring.
- Spray paint the structure. Apply two coats.
- On the brass wire, put a tip, crush, and then thread the pendants and attach the whole piece to the chandelier (see drawing).
- In the center of the lamp, attach a flat cabochon with pendants in such a way that a votive candle can be placed on top of it.
- Attach a faceted cabochon above the candle to "distribute" the light.

Vine Stock Chandelier

TIME: 2.5 HOURS + DRYING

I HAD A SOFT SPOT FOR THIS CLASSIC WAX-ENCRUSTED "HORROR MUSEUM" PIECE INHERITED FROM THE RURAL WORLD. REDEEMING ITS NOBILITY WAS A REAL CHALLENGE.

41

Materials

- 1 chandelier with vine base
- Chandelier beads and pendants
- Small faceted white beads
- Tips
- Brass wire
- 1 jar of matte white paint
- 1 brush
- 1 spatula
- 1 pair of rubber gloves
- 1 drill
- Pliers

Directions

- Rinse the chandelier under hot water. Protect your hands with rubber gloves. Remove any leftover wax from earlier use with your spatula. Let dry.
- Drill several holes in the candle ring.
- Paint the vine base with several coats of matte white paint. Let dry.
- Put a tip on the brass wire and crush with the pliers. Thread a small faceted white bead and a few crystal chandelier beads. String about 2 feet of white faceted beads. Finish the end in the same way as the beginning.
- You will need to double the brass wire for the chandelier pendants and beads that you attach to the candle ring.

TIME: 1.5 HOURS + DRYING

Materials
- 3 sconces with unmatched pendants
- Mount boards
- Wood lintels
- 6 strands of beads
- Small candles
- Bluish-gray paint
- 1 fat brush
- Nails
- 1 hammer

Sconce with Pendants

SCONCES GET A FRESH START WHEN THEY ARE REFASHIONED.

AS YOU TRANSFORM THEM, THEY CAN BE MADE BOTH RUSTIC

AND REFINED BY PLAYING OFF THE CONTRAST IN MATERIALS.

Directions
- Assemble the board using the lintels for support. Paint bluish-gray.
- Remove the sconce wiring.
- Nail the sconces to the boards.
- In order to hide the other wiring, place strands of beads on the candle rings. They'll help diffuse the candlelight.
- Place the candles at the center of the sconces.

LOIN DE TOI
L'IMPUR,
LE PROFANE,
PAIN RÉSERVÉ
POUR LES ENFANTS
METS DES ÉLUS,
CÉLESTE MANNE,
OBJET SEUL
DIGNE DE NOS CHANTS

ECCE PANIS
ANGELORUM

FACTUS

CIBUS

Baroque Candlestick

HOW CAN YOU MAKE A BAROQUE CANDLESTICK FROM A BASIC

GASLIGHT? IT'S AS EASY AS BUYING A CANDLE! THE GASLIGHT WAS

TURNED UPSIDE DOWN AND THE SHADE WAS ATTACHED TO

WHERE THE CANDLE IS PLACED!

INDIAN FARMERS SCULPT THEIR SEEDERS THEMSELVES. WHEN HUNG UPSIDE DOWN FROM THE NECKS OF THEIR COWS, THE SEEDS FALL THROUGH THE THREE LITTLE HOLES. SO THE ANIMAL SOWS WHILE WALKING. ALL YOU HAVE TO DO IS TURN THE SEEDER OVER AND INSERT THE CANDLES.

Seed Merchant's Candleholder

Materials
- 1 1950s lantern
- 1 large sheet of wax paper
- Copper leaf
- Newspaper
- 1 round brush
- Adhesive spray

TIME: 1.5 HOURS

Wrought Iron Lantern

ONCE YOU TAKE OUT THE PANES FROM THE LANTERN, YOU CAN APPRECIATE THE ELEGANCE OF THE IRON CURLICUES. IN ORDER TO GIVE THEM SOME LIFE AND GRACE, I CHOSE TO USE WAX PAPER, GILDED WITH GOLD LEAF.

Directions
- Remove the panes of pebbled glass from the light fixture.
- Make a template out of a sheet of newspaper. Cut four pieces of wax paper.
- Still using the newspaper, make a mask in an original shape or stencil. Spray the glue.
- Apply the copper leaf using a round brush.
- Glue the wax paper pieces to the armature.

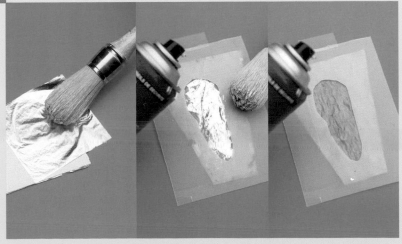

Floor Lamp
with Arabesques

I LIKED THE "COZY" ENGLISH FEEL OF THIS FLOOR LAMP. THE BIRDCAGE, BOTH

QUAINT AND ELEGANT, ADDS A SPECIAL TOUCH AND GIVES IT A COUNTRY FLAIR.

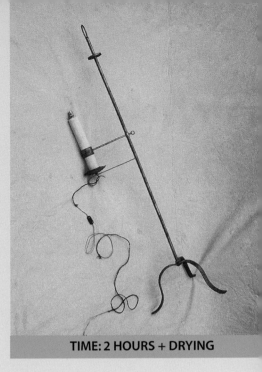

TIME: 2 HOURS + DRYING

Materials
- 1 lamp from a secondhand store
- 1 lampshade
- Antique-gold or red-gold paint
- White paint
- 1 small jar of bronze model paint
- 1 small jar of gold model paint
- 1 piece of wood
- 1 brush

Directions
- Strip the piece of wood if it's covered in wax and paint white.
- Paint the lamp gold.
- Paint bronze arabesques on the white lampshade. Highlight with gold.
- Rewire the lamp.

Filling with Furniture...

Eclectic and colorful, a cheerful medley of great finds …

TIME: 4 HOURS + DRYING

Materials

- 1 second-hand pedestal table
- Green velvet ribbon with trim border
- Metal (or fabric) roses in different colors and sizes
- Small and large, golden-brown faceted beads
- Metal head pins
- Small upholstery tacks
- Pistachio-green paint
- Fuchsia paint
- Thinner
- 1 brush
- 1 hammer
- Pliers
- Glue

"Couture" Pedestal Table

MADE OF DIFFERENT KINDS OF WOOD, THIS QUAINT, PLAIN TABLE TURNS

INTO A VERY "COUTURE" PIECE OF FURNITURE. LACQUERED IN PISTACHIO

GREEN AND DOTTED WITH FUCHSIA, IT WILL LIGHT UP YOUR LIVING ROOM.

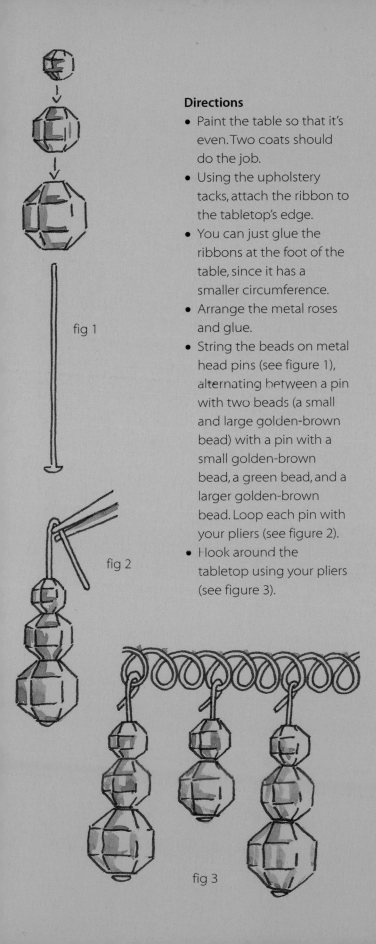

fig 1

fig 2

fig 3

Directions

- Paint the table so that it's even. Two coats should do the job.
- Using the upholstery tacks, attach the ribbon to the tabletop's edge.
- You can just glue the ribbons at the foot of the table, since it has a smaller circumference.
- Arrange the metal roses and glue.
- String the beads on metal head pins (see figure 1), alternating between a pin with two beads (a small and large golden-brown bead) with a pin with a small golden-brown bead, a green bead, and a larger golden-brown bead. Loop each pin with your pliers (see figure 2).
- Hook around the tabletop using your pliers (see figure 3).

Breakfast Tray

ADD TWO HANDLES, A DRAWER KNOB, AND SOME PAINT TO A

SMALL CHILDREN'S TABLE AND YOU'LL HAVE A SUNDAY MORNING

BREAKFAST TRAY.

TIME: 1.5 HOURS + DRYING

Materials
- 1 salvaged table
- Prayer strips in Sanskrit
- 2 handles
- 1 drawer knob
- Basque red paint
- Purple paint
- Adhesive spray
- 1 saw

Directions
- Shorten the table legs with the saw.
- Paint the little table in Basque red and purple.
- Use the adhesive spray to glue the prayer scrolls.
- Attach a handle on each side of the tray. Attach the drawer knob.

Period Chair

THIS CHAIR WITH A REMOVABLE SEAT IS A GODSEND! BLACK QUARTZ COVERED WITH A SHEET OF THICK PLEXIGLAS ADDS FLASH AND SPARKLE TO THIS OLD CHAIR.

TIME: 10 MINUTES

Materials
- Black quartz
- Sheet of Plexiglas cut to size

Directions
- Fill the seat with quartz.
- Carefully put down the cut Plexiglas

A Short History of Wrought Iron

The Hittites, the people of Caucasus, were the first to develop the technique of iron reduction about 1700–1500 B.C. Only a few arms and tools have survived from this far-off time, the thinnest pieces having been destroyed by oxidation. The ancient Egyptians hardly used iron since they didn't have forests to produce the charcoal, which was indispensable to reducing ore. Later, Gaul was a major supplier: today we use the same tool-making techniques (for hammers, axes, saws, tongs, pincers, trowels, etc.) developed by the Gauls. Wrought iron work flourished during the Middle Ages when all the abbeys placed importance on forges. Italian models were adopted during the Renaissance and heralded Louis XIV classicism. But, it was under the reign of Louis XV that wrought iron work reached its zenith in chancels in churches and park gates, building doors, balconies, banisters, and more. When casting was developed in 1750, wrought iron practice lost popularity, but today, outside the industrial sector, the art of wrought iron work is being honored in original pieces and in restoration projects.

BECAUSE OF THE AIRY STRUCTURE OF WROUGHT IRON, WE CAN PLAY WITH SOLID FORMS, SLENDER SHAPES, AND TRANSPARENCY. LET'S MAKE TWO VERSIONS OF THIS TABLE; ONE WITH CUT SLATE AND THE OTHER WITH WORKED RESIN FOR A MORE REFINED LOOK.

TIME: 3 HOURS

"Madame" Table

Materials

- Chandelier pendants in various sizes
- Fake cultured pearls
- A piece of slate
- Brass wire
- Gold spray paint
- Screwdriver

For the refined version:

- Cernit or Fimo polymer clay
- White imitation gems
- White gouache
- Dark or light gold model paint
- 2 tips
- Pliers

Directions
- Spray paint the table structure.
- Hang the pendants using the brass wire. Alternate with small and large pendants (see figure 1).
- Put a tip on the wire. String the fake cultured pearls. Complete with another tip. Arrange around the perimeter of the tabletop (see figure 2).

For the cut slate version:
- Cover the tabletop with pieces of slate to play off the contrast between the raw aspect of the slate and the Baroque character of the gold, pearls, and pendants. Cutting slate is fairly easy.
- Using a screwdriver, mark the slate where it is to be cut by pressing down firmly. Then, place the slate along the edge of a piece of furniture. Break off the piece by pushing down assertively.

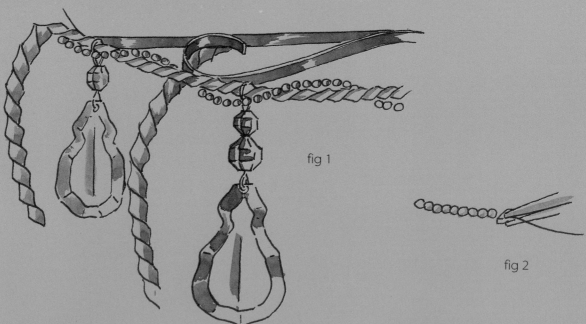

fig 1

fig 2

For the refined version:

- Knead small quantities of the polymer clay until you have a large ball.
- Roll out a square that is the same size as the tabletop. Add more clay if necessary to even out surface.
- Once you have a square, stamp the surface with the ornaments of your choice (buttons, stones, etc.).
- While the clay is still soft, insert imitation gems into the clay that match the pendants.
- Bake in the oven for 20 minutes at the appropriate temperature (250 or 300° F).
- Once it has cooled, brush white gouache onto stamped areas. Let dry.
- Clean the surface of the piece with a lightly dampened rag, so that white remains only in the depressions.
- Use a rag to apply the dark gold paint. Blot the excess. Highlight the reliefs with light gold so that it goes with the gold of the wrought iron.
- Place on the tabletop and glue.

Nineteenth Century Wrought Iron Bed

WHETHER YOU PUT IT UNDER YOUR GARDEN CHERRY TREE, WHERE IT WILL BE DAPPLED WITH SUNLIGHT, OR COVER IT WITH BEAUTIFUL BLANKETS AND QUILTS, HERE ARE TWO VERSIONS OF THIS PORTABLE BED, ONE FOR WINTER AND ONE FOR SUMMER.

Turquoise Table

FOR MONTHS IT REMAINED IN THE

SECONDHAND SHOP WITH ITS BROWN TILES,

WRAPPED IN PACKAGING TAPE, WAITING FOR

A POTENTIAL BUYER. WITH A FEW STROKES OF

MAGIC PAINT, IT FOUND A HOME NEAR THE

COUCH ONCE AGAIN.

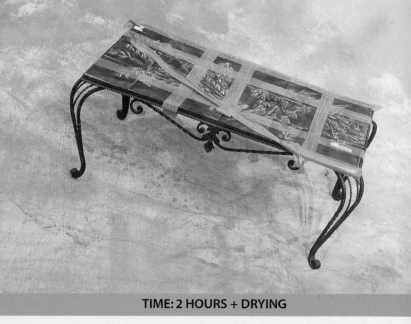

TIME: 2 HOURS + DRYING

Materials

- 1 wrought iron coffee table
- 1 sheet of plywood to be cut by a carpenter
- Turquoise paint
- Matte black paint
- Thinner
- Brushes

Directions

- Remove the old tiles. Strip the wrought iron armature and clean with water.
- Once dry, bring out its beauty by painting it matte black.
- Paint the pre-cut board in turquoise blue. Several coats will be necessary (about three).
- You can make a second version by painting the other side of the board. Use a different color or decorate it.

"Stendhal" Chair

A DAY OF PASSION! I BOUGHT THIS CHAIR ONE MORNING, AND

TRANSFORMED IT BY DINNERTIME. PASSION IN RED AND BLACK ...

A WHOLE NOVEL!

TIME: 1 HOUR + DRYING

Materials
- Imitation leather chair found at the flea market
- Black spray paint
- Dark red Cernit or Fimo polymer clay
- 1 small jar of gold model paint
- Stylo
- Glue

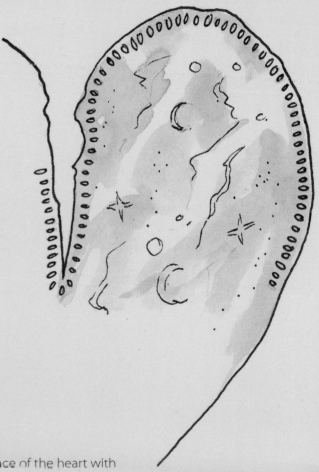

Directions
- Spray paint the chair matte black. Apply three coats.
- Knead the polymer clay for about 15 minutes and roll out into a 5 x 5-inch square.
- Use the stylo to cut out a heart.
- Decorate the surface of the heart with stamps of your choice. Bake in the oven for 20 minutes at the required temperature, (250 or 300° F).
- Paint the stamped areas with gold. Wipe.
- Glue the heart on the seat back.

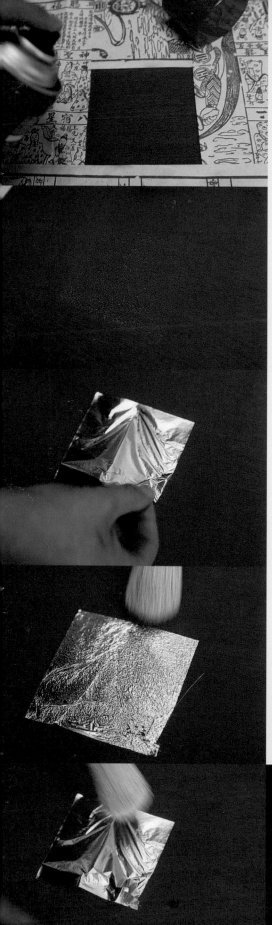

Materials

- Iron rack
- Wood base and side panels cut to size by a carpenter
- 4 copper leaves, (3.5 x 4 in.)
- Red paint
- 1 brush
- Adhesive spray

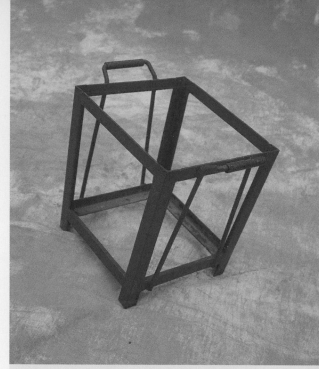

TIME: 2 HOURS + DRYING

Wood Crate

YOU CAN PURCHASE AN IRON RACK FOR NEXT TO NOTHING.

THE COPPER LEAF AGAINST THE RED WILL GIVE A JAPANESE FEEL.

Directions

- Paint the base and side panels in red. Let dry and apply a second coat.
- Cut a square the size of the copper leaf out of newspaper. Spray glue through the cutout onto the crate.
- Apply the copper leaf using a fat brush.
- Repeat steps on other panels.

TIME: 1.5 HOURS

Materials
- 1 old table from a secondhand store
- 1 salvaged plank of thick wood
- 1 old slab of zinc from a scrap dealer
- Wax
- Glue

Zinc Table

FIND HARMONY IN ASYMMETRY.

THIS IS THE MOTTO OF DESIGNERS

TODAY. IN THIS CASE, THE UNTREATED

ZINC TABLETOP IS JUXTAPOSED

AGAINST AN ELEGANT TABLE BASE,

BRINGING TOGETHER THE BAROQUE

AND THE PRIMITIVE.

Directions
- Because zinc is difficult to work with, it's better to have a zinc worker cover the slab (allow for 1 hour of work).
- Glue the piece onto the base.
- Apply beeswax to the zinc to nourish it.

Materials

- 1 jardinière
- Matte white paint
- Bronze spray paint
- 1 jar of gold model paint
- Gold sparkles
- Small plants of your choice
- Candlesticks from the secondhand store
- Candles
- 25 pounds of dishwashing salts
- 1 brush

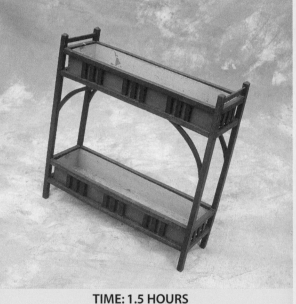

TIME: 1.5 HOURS

Designer Jardinière

DISTINCTIVELY ROMANTIC, A JARDINIÈRE WILL GIVE

CITY TERRACES AND GARDENS THE FEEL OF AN

OPEN-AIR CAFÉ.

Directions

- Give the wood structure two coats of paint in a nice matte white.
- Paint the zinc flower boxes bronze.
- Sponge with gold paint to give the boxes a crackled, aged look.
- Distribute the 25 pounds of salts in the flower boxes.
- Arrange the candlesticks and houseplants.
- Sprinkle with sparkles for a candlelight dinner.

To decorate...

With a light touch, patience, and a lot of imagination, transform the object ... and make it your own.

Materials

- Anise green felt
- 1-inch-wide purple ribbon
- 1.5-inch-wide gold trim
- Old or antique trim
- 2 antique-gold tassels
- 2 silver beads
- 2 amethyst beads
- 2 purple pâte-de-verre glass beads
- Anise green thread
- Needle

Tea Cozy

FOR YOU TEA LOVERS, A TEA COZY IS A GREAT

AND INDISPENSABLE ACCESSORY. BOTH

ATTRACTIVE AND PRACTICAL, IT RETAINS THE

WARMTH OF THE *1001 NIGHTS*!

TIME: 3 HOURS

Directions
- Cut a template the size of the teapot out of newspaper.
- Place on top of the felt and cut out two pieces. Sew together.
- Sew the purple ribbon along the seam. Add the 1.5-inch ribbon as a finishing touch.
- Sew the antique trim along the bottom of the cozy.
- Double your thread and string the tassel, the silver bead, the amethyst, and the purple beads. Sew to the middle of the rounded edge. Follow the same steps on the other side.

89

Table Runner

THIS GRATING STOPS LEAVES FROM CLOGGING THE GUTTER. WITH THREE

OF THESE OBJECTS FROM YOUR SCRAP-METAL DEALER, SOME IVY, COFFEE

BEANS, AND A FEW CANDLES, YOU CAN WELCOME YOUR FRIENDS WITH

AN EXOTIC TOUCH.

TIME: 15 MINUTES

Bottle Rack

SO SIMPLE ... A FEW DIFFERENT-SHAPED BLUE

BOTTLES AND AN IRON RACK WITH THE PATINA OF

AGE ARE ALL YOU NEED TO MAKE AN ORIGINAL

COUNTRY BOUQUET.

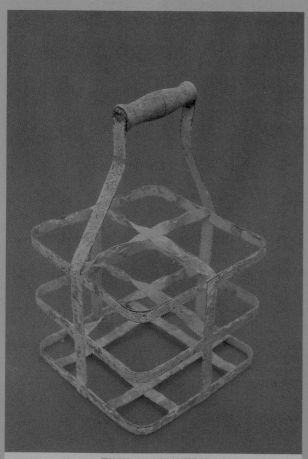

TIME: 10 MINUTES

Materials

- Black Cernit or Fimo polymer clay
- 1 fishing lure
- 1 piece of 2 x 2.5 inch Canson paper
- Ultramarine pigments and varnish
- Antique-gold paint
- Gold sparkles
- Glue

TIME: 1.5 HOURS

IN THE 1960s, YVES KLEIN, THE PAINTER, AND ADAM, THE CHEMICAL RETAILER, MADE A SPECIAL SOLUTION THAT RETAINED THE BRILLIANCY OF THE ULTRAMARINE PIGMENT, CREATING WHAT IS KNOWN TODAY AS INTERNATIONAL KLEIN BLUE. IT IS IN THIS HARMONY OF BLUE THAT OUR FISH IS IMMERSED.

Klein Blue Frame

Directions

- Knead the polymer clay little by little for about 15 minutes. Once well softened, roll out into a 4 x 4.5-inch rectangle. Inside, cut out a 2 x 2.5-inch rectangle, and remove.
- Decorate the smaller rectangle with inlay of your choice
- Bake in the oven for 20 minutes at the appropriate temperature (250 or 300° F). Let cool.
- In the meantime, mix the ultramarine pigments and the varnish.

- Paint the 2 x 2.5-inch sheet of Canson paper Klein blue.
- Saturate the rough surface of the frame with the same mix. Wipe.
- Finish the frame with antique-gold paint and wipe with a rag to make it look old.
- Coat the rough surface around the central square with glue and sprinkle with sparkles.
- Glue the Klein blue rectangle to the back of the frame.
- To finish, remove the hook and glue the lure.

Antique Vase

COVER AN EVERYDAY TAPERED VASE WITH COATING

AND BRONZE FINISH, ADD A FEW GOLD LEAVES, AND

THE COMMON BECOMES A MUSEUM PIECE.

TIME: 2 HOURS + DRYING

Materials
- 1 simple terracotta vase
- Quick-dry coating
- Black paint
- Green-bronze antique finish
- Copper leaf
- 1 old toothbrush
- 1 spatula
- 1 brush
- Glue

Directions
- Using the spatula, cover the vase with quick-dry coating.
- Work the surface with imprints of your choice.
- Once the vase is dry, apply two coats of black paint and let dry.
- Using an old toothbrush, apply the green-bronze antique finish.

- Cover the top and bottom of the vase, leaving an approximately 4-inch strip in the middle. Apply glue to this strip and then to the copper leaf, dabbing it with a fat brush.

Springtime Pedestal Table

THIS SIMPLE GARDEN TABLE, RUSTED BY TIME,

CLIMBED THE RANKS AND BECAME A

MONUMENTAL TRIPOD FOR AN ANTIQUE VASE.

UNTIL THE NEXT TRANSFORMATION....

TIME: 1.5 HOURS

"Arte Povera" Frame

NOTHING GOES TO WASTE, EVERYTHING HAS THE POTENTIAL

TO BECOME SOMETHING ELSE. YOUR RUSTED TABLE CAN BE A

WORK OF ART. JUST TAKE CHOCOLATE WRAPPER, GLUE A FEW

SPARKLES TO THE BACK OF YOUR RUST-EATEN METAL, AND

SECURE THE PIECE BETWEEN TWO PANES OF GLASS.

Primitive Shield

A WHEEL FROM A ROMAN CHARIOT OR A

MEDIEVAL CART ... THIS ANCIENT OBJECT

SPARKED MY IMAGINATION AND IT COST NEXT

TO NOTHING AT THE SECONDHAND STORE. THE

DEALER WAS JUST THRILLED TO GET RID OF THE

60 POUNDS OF WOOD AND SCRAP IRON! A VERY

SUBSTANTIAL DECORATING IDEA FOR PLAYING

WITH SHADOWS AGAINST A WHITE WALL.

Fabric Rack

I FOUND THIS LADDER ON

THE STREET ON THE NIGHT

THEY COLLECT BULK ITEMS

AND GAVE IT A HOME

AGAINST MY LIVING ROOM

WALL. THE RAW LOOK OF

THE DRIFTWOOD GOES

WELL WITH THE FINE

FABRICS.

Travel Trunk

THE OLD TRUNK AND THE MUNITIONS BOX

WERE WORKED ON IN THE SAME SPIRIT SO THAT

THEY WOULD FORM A SET. THE POSTCARD OF A

POMPEII FRESCO WAS ADDED TO SUGGEST

BOTH ANTIQUITY AND TRAVEL SOUVENIRS.

TIME: 3 HOURS + DRYING

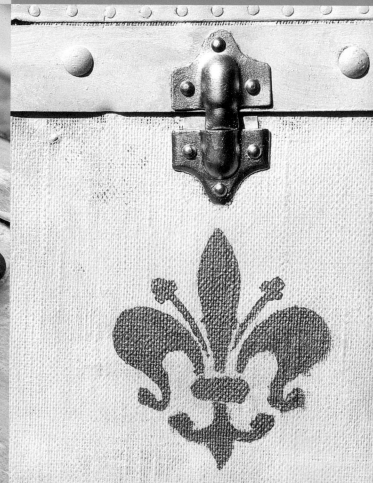

MUNITIONS BOX

Materials

- 1 old box
- 1 postcard of a fresco
- 1 braided trim
- 1 carved cuttlefish bone with imitation gems
- 1 tassel
- Matte white spray paint
- Upholstery tacks
- 1 hammer

Directions

- Apply two coats of spray paint to the box.
- Glue the postcard to the top of box and the trim around the edge. Tack the four corners.
- On the front of the box, attach the carved cuttlefish bone with two tacks.
- Attach the tassel in the same way.

TRUNK

Materials
- 1 old trunk
- 1 fleur-de-lis stencil
- Matte white paint
- 1 small jar of bronze model paint
- 1 small jar of gold model paint
- 1 fat round brush
- 1 thin brush

Directions
- Paint the inside and the outside of the trunk. Apply two coats.
- Let it dry, then paint the metal bands in bronze.
- Dab with gold paint to give it an old look.
- At the bottom of the trunk, apply the stencil. Apply a first coat of bronze and highlight with light gold.

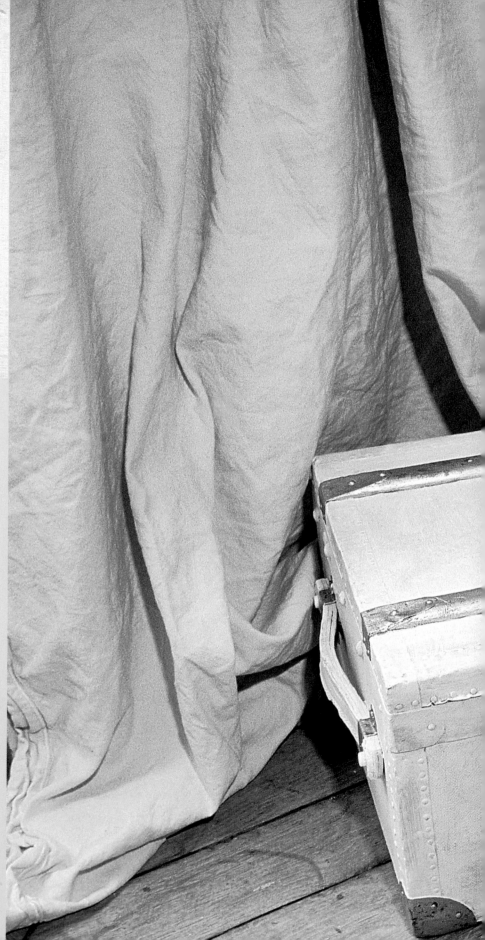

Gift Box

WITH ITS ENGRAVING AND FINISH, THIS WOODEN BOX CAN BE USED FOR CANDY OR JEWELRY. A HEART PLACED INSIDE WILL SAY "I LOVE YOU. COME BACK TO ME."

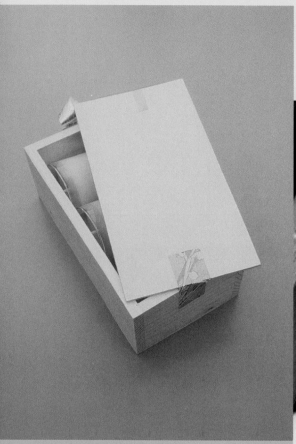

TIME: 1.5 HOURS

Materials
- 1 soft wood box
- 1 wood-burning pen
- 1 small jar of bronze model paint
- White paint
- 1 old toothbrush
- 1 rag

Directions

- On a soft wood box, engrave simple designs, even dots, as seen here.
- Saturate with bronze paint to give it relief. Let dry.
- Using a toothbrush, cover with white paint. Wipe. You can present your gift on a small handmade cushion made from a piece of taffeta filled with kapok, like in the model.

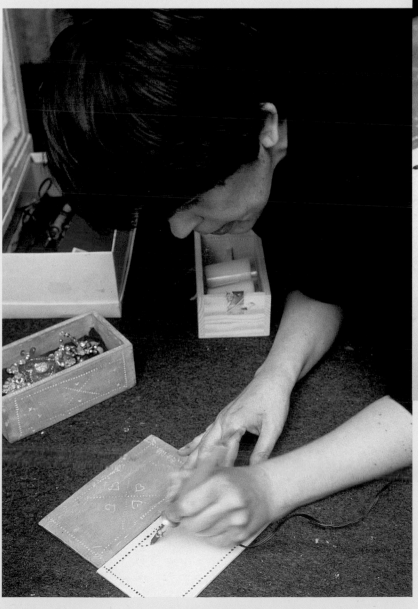

Bracelet
Display

THIS OLD CLAMP HAS A NEW LIFE AS A DISPLAY

RACK FOR BRACELETS AND PRIMITIVE JEWELRY.

Jewelry Box

A CARDBOARD CANDY BOX COVERED IN UPHOLSTERY

FABRIC WAS A MUST-HAVE ITEM IN THE 1960S. IT HAS A

FRESH SPIN AS A MEDIEVAL CHEST.

TIME: 3.5 HOURS

Materials
- Gold paint
- Antique-gold trim
- 1 metal-thread tassel
- 1 curved metal piece decorated with openwork
- 1 gold paper doily
- Medium-size jet-black beads
- Small, antique-gold beads
- Turquoise beads
- Round and oblong red imitation gems
- 1 needle
- Brown thread
- Gold wire
- Glue

119

Directions

- Paint with a brush or spray paint the box gold.
- Glue the antique-gold trim on top of the trim that is already there, now gold, to add relief.
- Sew the jet beads along the bottom of the box. Use the brown thread, which won't be seen on the antique-gold trim, instead of the gold thread, which is much more fragile.
- On the top of the box, arrange the sewn jet beads, the turquoise beads and the glued red imitation gems in sequence.
- In the middle of the box, glue the gold paper doily. Border with antique-gold trim. Then sew and glue the jet beads, the turquoise beads, and the red imitation gems.
- Thread beads on the wire and attach to the curved metal piece decorated with openwork. Arrange so that the piece's shape is accentuated.
- Use wire to attach the tassel to the back of the piece.
- Glue both to box.

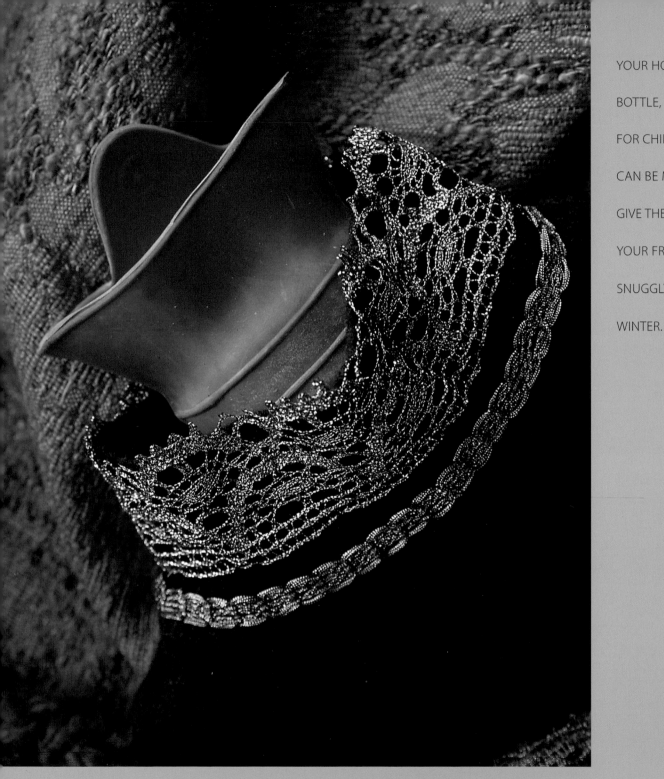

YOUR HOT-WATER

BOTTLE, ESSENTIAL

FOR CHILLY NIGHTS,

CAN BE MADE SOFT.

GIVE THEM TO ALL

YOUR FRIENDS FOR A

SNUGGLY-CHIC

WINTER.

Hot-Water Bottle Cover

Materials:

- 1 old and thick boiled-wool sweater with a high round neck
- 3 kinds of old trim
- 1 piece of blood-red velvet fabric
- 1 thread-wrapped bead
- 1 pair of scissors
- Brown thread
- 1 needle

TIME: 3 HOURS

fig 1

Directions

- Slide the hot water bottle into the sweater to check the size.
- Cut around the hot water bottle. Now that the wool has been cut, it looks like felt and won't fray. Take out the hot water bottle.
- Edge the turtleneck with wide trimming ribbon. Because gold thread is too delicate, use brown thread, which won't show in the antique-gold trim. Sew a thinner ribbon beneath it.
- Do the same along the bottom of the sweater.
- On a sheet of paper, draw a heart for the hot water bottle. Place it on the velvet and cut it out.
- Place the heart in the middle using pins, then sew the trim around the edge, the lace facing out. Once you have done this, sew another row, lace facing in (see figures 1 and 2).

fig 2

1900 Frame

HAVING REMOVED THE PICTURE, THIS FRAME BECOMES A PIECE OF ART IN ITSELF, WHETHER IT'S PLACED AGAINST AN OLD TAPESTRY OR AROUND ANOTHER FRAME USED TO EMBELLISH A NEAPOLITAN COMMEMORATIVE PLAQUE.

Commemorative Temple

HAPPY DAY OF THE

DEAD! THIS TEMPLE

IS LIKE THE MEXICAN

ONES, BOTH IN ITS

EXECUTION AND

PRESENTATION, WITH

A NOD TO MYSTICAL

JOURNEYS.

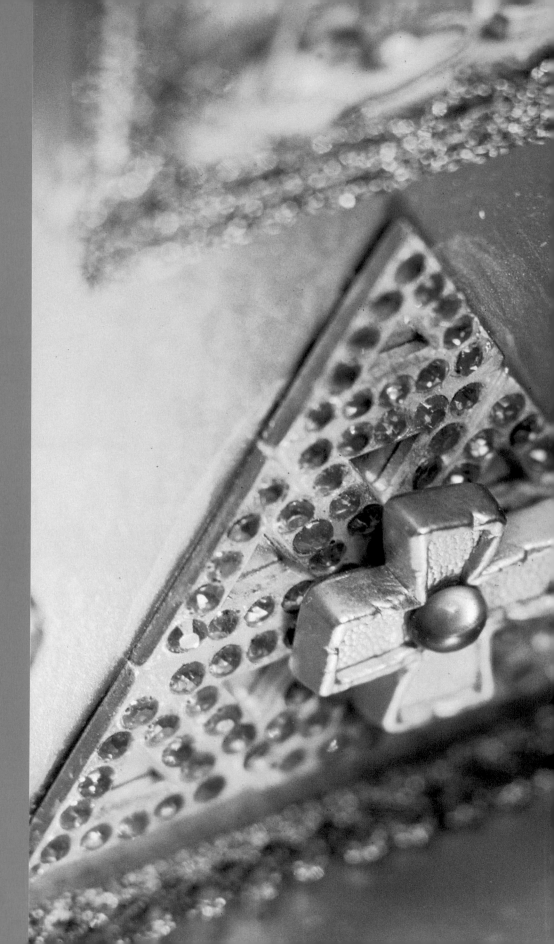

Materials

- 1 cardboard box measuring 6 x 6 inches, complete with cover
- 1 piece of cardboard to make the pediment.
- 2 cardboard tubes from fax paper rolls
- Antique trim of different sizes and designs
- 1 postcard of an icon or religious portrait
- Colored tissue paper, photos from a magazine for the scenes framing the main image
- Gold and red chocolate wrapper
- Pieces of broken jewelry
- Buttons
- Earrings
- 2 faceted glass cabochons (from chandelier pendants)
- Gold spray paint
- Glue

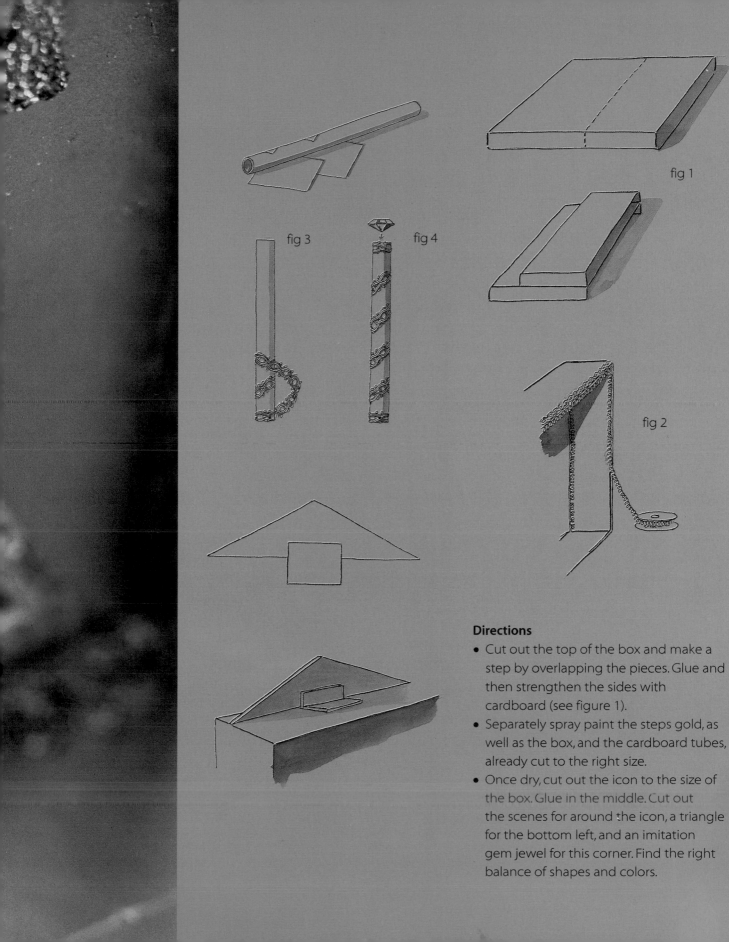

fig 1

fig 3

fig 4

fig 2

Directions

- Cut out the top of the box and make a step by overlapping the pieces. Glue and then strengthen the sides with cardboard (see figure 1).
- Separately spray paint the steps gold, as well as the box, and the cardboard tubes, already cut to the right size.
- Once dry, cut out the icon to the size of the box. Glue in the middle. Cut out the scenes for around the icon, a triangle for the bottom left, and an imitation gem jewel for this corner. Find the right balance of shapes and colors.

- Once you have found harmony, glue the scenes or the jewelry pieces (like the triangle) around the icon.
- Edge the icon and the scenes with trimming ribbon. Glue.
- Glue ribbon along the walls and back of the box (figure 2).
- Glue broken pieces of jewelry or buttons to the middle of some of the scenes.
- Glue imitation gems to the trim around the icon and on some of the scenes. Then place it on top of the steps. Glue.
- On the gold cardboard tubes, glue gold chocolate wrapper and then wrap trim around it (see figure 3).
- Attach the columns in front of the temple and glue a faceted glass cabochon on top for decoration (see figure 4).
- For the pediment, cut a triangle out of the cardboard the size of the box. Glue a cardboard rectangle, which will act as a prop, to the back of the pediment (see figure 4). Paint the roof gold.
- Cut out a diamond-shape and colorful scene. Place and glue in a piece of broken jewelry. Edge completely with trim, then glue an imitation gem on top.
- Edge the triangle with trim. Glue it to the box.
- Glue the wide trimming ribbon to the base. Glue the cultured pearl earrings on top.
- Hang earring pieces from the trim.
- Glue pieces of old jewelry to the middle of the steps.
- For the miniature candle, cut a votive candle into little squares and wrap in red chocolate wrapper.

When you're going out...

A beautiful bohemian, touched by the fairy wand and dressed in little whatnots, goes out to dance at the ball …

Day Bag

ANYONE WHO HAS SOME

STYLE WILL TELL YOU

THE SAME THING:

ACCESSORIES CHANGE

EVERYTHING. FROM

THE SIMPLE, PRACTICAL

BAG TO THE VALENTINE'S

HEART BAG . . . THE

POSSIBILITIES ARE

ENDLESS.

Materials

- A half yard of crushed velvet + a small piece of crushed velvet in another color for the heart.
- ½ yard of satin lining
- 2 kinds of antique trim
- 2 large tassels
- 1 medium tassel
- 1 button
- 2 small roses made of colored metal
- Beads from an old necklace
- 7 x 7.5 inch rectangle cut from a padded envelope.

TIME: 5 HOURS SEWN BY HAND

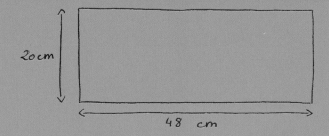

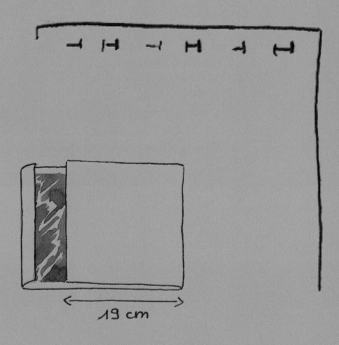

Directions

- Cut an 8 x 19-inch rectangle out of the crushed velvet and the satin lining. Sew them edge to edge. Before completing the sewing, insert the padded envelope rectangle to stiffen the bag.
- Then, fold over 7.5 inches of fabric to close up the bag (see figure). The bubble wrap should fold over the back of the bag. Pin or baste the piece.
- Place the trim to decorate the bag and sew along the edge, including the shoulder strap.
- Using a template to guarantee the proportions, cut a heart out of the other piece of velvet. Secure it with pins, set down the trim around it, and sew.

- Sew the tassels at the bottom of the bag and the roses on top.
- Place trim along the flap. Then, stitch on colored beads. In the middle, sew the button and the tassel as a clasp.
- Arrange the necklace pieces as indicated in the model. Play with the heart, as shown here, by sewing one inside the big one using a piece of trim. Glue a rose on top for decoration.

Materials

- 1 yard of red and purple moiré fabric
- 1 black sweater, boiled
- 1 gold trimming ribbon with openwork
- 1.5 yards of antique-gold cord
- 1 secondhand pin
- 1 bead-and-chain antique tassel
- Purple thread
- 1 ribbon that matches the fabric

A CONE WITH TAFFETA

FRILLS AND DECORATED

WITH OLD JEWELRY

WILL BE THE PERFECT

TOUCH TO AN EVENING

DRESS. NIGHTTIME IS

MEANT FOR

EXTRAVAGANCE.

TIME: 4 HOURS

Evening Bag

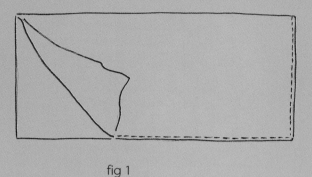

fig 1

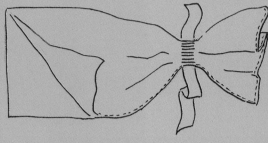

fig 2

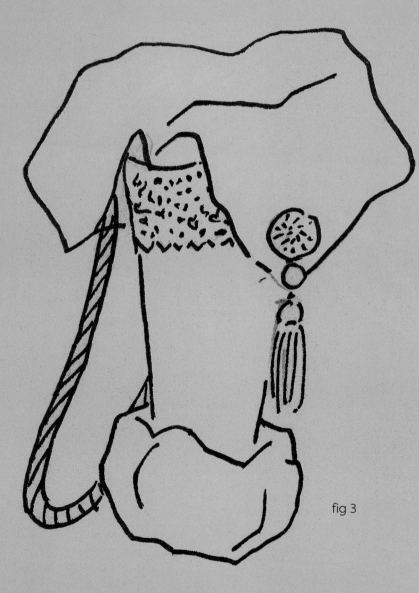

fig 3

Directions

- Cut out a sweater sleeve. Edge the two ends with gold trimming ribbon decorated with openwork.
- Sew the antique-gold cord to the inside of the sleeve as a shoulder strap.
- Make a 22 x 24-inch rectangle with a double layer of moiré fabric and sew.
- Then, fold the 22-inch side over, making a 11 x 24 inch rectangle. Sew this rectangle three-quarters of the way so that you have a big flap (see figure 1).
- About a third of the way from the bottom, cinch and sew what will be the bottom of the bag. Cover the thread with the ribbon that matches the moiré fabric (see figure 2).
- Slip the whole piece into the sleeve and turn up the fabric around the bottom of the bag (see figure 3).
- Roll down the top into an elegant and asymmetrical cuff. Using the pin, which has been decorated with the tassel, clip the corner of the fabric to the soft wool.

Materials

- 1 inexpensive pair of shoes
- 2 kinds of antique trimming ribbon
- 1 purple ribbon
- Brass wire
- Tips
- Small and shimmering purple beads
- Pistachio-green oblong beads
- Glue
- Pliers
- 1 needle and thread

Embroidered Mules

EVERYONE DREAMS OF BEING GLAMOUR GAL FOR A NIGHT

(OR A WEEK OR A YEAR). WITH THESE PEARL-EMBROIDERED

MULES, IT CAN COME TRUE.

TIME: 2.5 HOURS

Directions:

- Cut about 6 inches of wire. Put on a tip and crush with your pliers. Then successively string purple and green beads. Adjust the length to the width of the shoe. Put on a tip and crush. Repeat these steps with two other wires.
- Cut a piece of purple ribbon, glue it, and then edge it with thin trimming ribbon for decoration.
- On either side of the wider strap, glue antique trimming ribbon.
- Glue or sew—whichever you prefer—the stringed beads.
- Repeat on the smaller strap.
- Do the same on the other shoe.

A Short History of Trim

*T*he art of trim, or "1001 ways to weave and interlace thread into little strips," has been around since prehistory. In its primitive form, plant fiber plaiting techniques were used that are similar to those adopted today. Before it was used for decoration, trim played a religious role: it was a kind of lucky charm against evil spells and misfortune. In ancient China, in Arabia, and Polynesia, it first emerged as a fringe, to which the Egyptians, Brazilian Indians, and Africans added feathers, shells, and colored beads.

With the development of shipping, trim quickly reached the Mediterranean area. Essentially made of wool and cotton thread during the Middle Ages, it was widespread in the Renaissance because of Italian art. From that point on, the European courts rivaled each other in splendor, wearing gold decorative details and woven silks. Louis XIV and his court were not an exception to this fashion. At the end of the eighteenth century, the French became the masters of trim, which they included in interior decoration. Then, with the industrial revolution, production became more democratic. Fabricated less expensively with textile machines, trim soon appeared in middle-class homes. Today, except in specific cases (military stripes, holy fabrics and classical tapestry work), trim has been brought back into style by fashion designers and interior decorators.

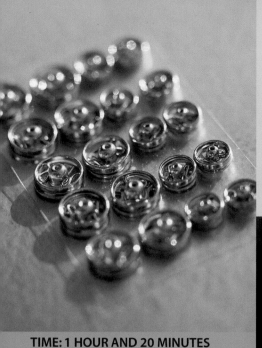

Materials

- 1 colored ribbon
- 1 antique-gold trimming ribbon decorated with openwork
- Beads of the same color as your ribbon
- Snaps
- Gold brass wire
- Tips
- Pliers

TIME: 1 HOUR AND 20 MINUTES

CREATE YOUR OWN

BEAUTIFUL BRACELETS

BY COMBINING

RIBBONS AND BEADS

OF YOUR CHOICE.

Trim Bracelets

Directions

- Cut the colored ribbon and the trim to the size of your wrist. Allow an extra inch for the finishing touches.
- Sew the ribbons together at the ends.
- Place the snap.
- Using the brass wire, dot the bracelet with beads (see figure).

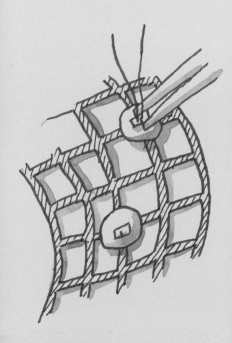

Acknowledgements

Thanks to:

Juliette Chanaud, Bertrand Cure, Carole Daprey, Caroline Dupouy, Christine and Gilles Gerry, Hervé Genty, Claudio Jacquemard, Christine Buchs, Sylvie Lebras, Sylvian and Jean-Paul Reboud.

I would like to thank all my friends who so graciously opened their homes and gardens.

I am eternally grateful to those who welcomed me to do my hunting all over France.

A big thanks to my daughter Caroline, who, from an early age, has been used to running around to the secondhand shops in France and Navarre, and who, with great joy, has helped me find many of the objects in this book.

Finally, thanks to Hervé Gentry, carpenter and journeyman, for having so graciously helped me make the zinc table.